GO Green

Having the
Energy

Helen Lanz

W
FRANKLIN WATTS
LONDON • SYDNEY

First published in 2010 by
Franklin Watts
338 Euston Road
London NW1 3BH

Franklin Watts Australia
Level 17/207 Kent Street
Sydney NSW 2000

Series editor: Julia Bird
Design: D.R. ink
Artworks: Mike Phillips

A CIP catalogue record for this book is available
from the British Library.

ISBN 978 0 7496 9272 8

Dewey classification: 337.7'9

Picture credits: Bestweb/Shutterstock: 20t; Michael Binson/Iconica/
Getty Images: 6; Bloomimages/Corbis: front cover t;
Helmut Meyer zur Capellen/imagebroker/Alamy: 3, 9t,
CECED: 15br; Paula Connelly/istockphoto: 11t; Rob Cruse/istockphoto: 11b.
Peter Elvidge/istockphoto: front cover b; Fotovoyager/istockphoto: 7tr.
Maciej Gowin/Shutterstock: 27; Chris Henderson/Construction Photography: 19t;
Jon Hicks/Alamy: 26; Image Source/Corbis: 16t; Israel Images/Alamy: 21b;
Darren Jenkins/Alamy: 22; Suzann Julien/istockphoto: 12b.
Edward Kinsman/SPL: 18; Daniel Leppens/istockphoto: 9b.
Lilun/Shutterstock: 7tl; Tim McCraig/istockphoto: 8b.
Nancy Durrell McKenna/Hutchison Archive/Alamy: 23t.
Jin Nan/epa/Corbis: 17b; Skip O'Donnell/istock[photo: 24t.
Bob Pearson/epa/Corbis: 11c; Konstantin Postumitenko/istockphoto: 15bl.
QH Photography/Shutterstock: 17tl; Robootb/Shutterstock: 20b.
RT Images/istockphoto: 19b; Stockbyte/Getty Images: 14.
Stephen Strathdee/istockphoto: 24b; Hüseyin Tuncer/istockphoto: 7b.
Pat Tuson/Alamy: 25; Tania Zbrodko/Shutterstock: 23b.

Every attempt has been made to clear copyright.
Should there be any inadvertent omission,
please apply to the publisher for rectification.

Printed in China

Franklin Watts is a division of Hachette Children's Books,
an Hachette UK company.
www.hachette.co.uk

To Charles - here's hoping for a surge of energy come triathlon day.

"*During 25 years of writing about the environment for the Guardian, I quickly realised that education was the first step to protecting the planet on which we all depend for survival. While the warning signs are everywhere that the Earth is heating up and the climate changing, many of us have been too preoccupied with living our lives to notice what is going on in our wider environment. It seems to me that it is children who need to know what is happening: they are often more observant of what is going on around them. We need to help them to grow up respecting and preserving the natural world on which their future depends. By teaching them about the importance of water, energy and other key areas of life, we can be sure they will soon be influencing their parents' lifestyles, too. This is a series of books every child should read.*"

Paul Brown
Former environment correspondent for *the Guardian*, environmental author and fellow of Wolfson College, Cambridge.

Contents page

Words in **bold** can be found in the glossary on page 28.

What is energy?

What have you done today? Did you walk to school or maybe go to the park on your scooter or bike? Whatever we do, it uses up our **energy**.

Food is fuel

Energy is the power we need to carry out an action or activity. Our energy comes from food. We need to eat a healthy, balanced diet so that our bodies can take the right amount of energy from it.

Eating the right food gives us the energy to do all the activities we want to do.

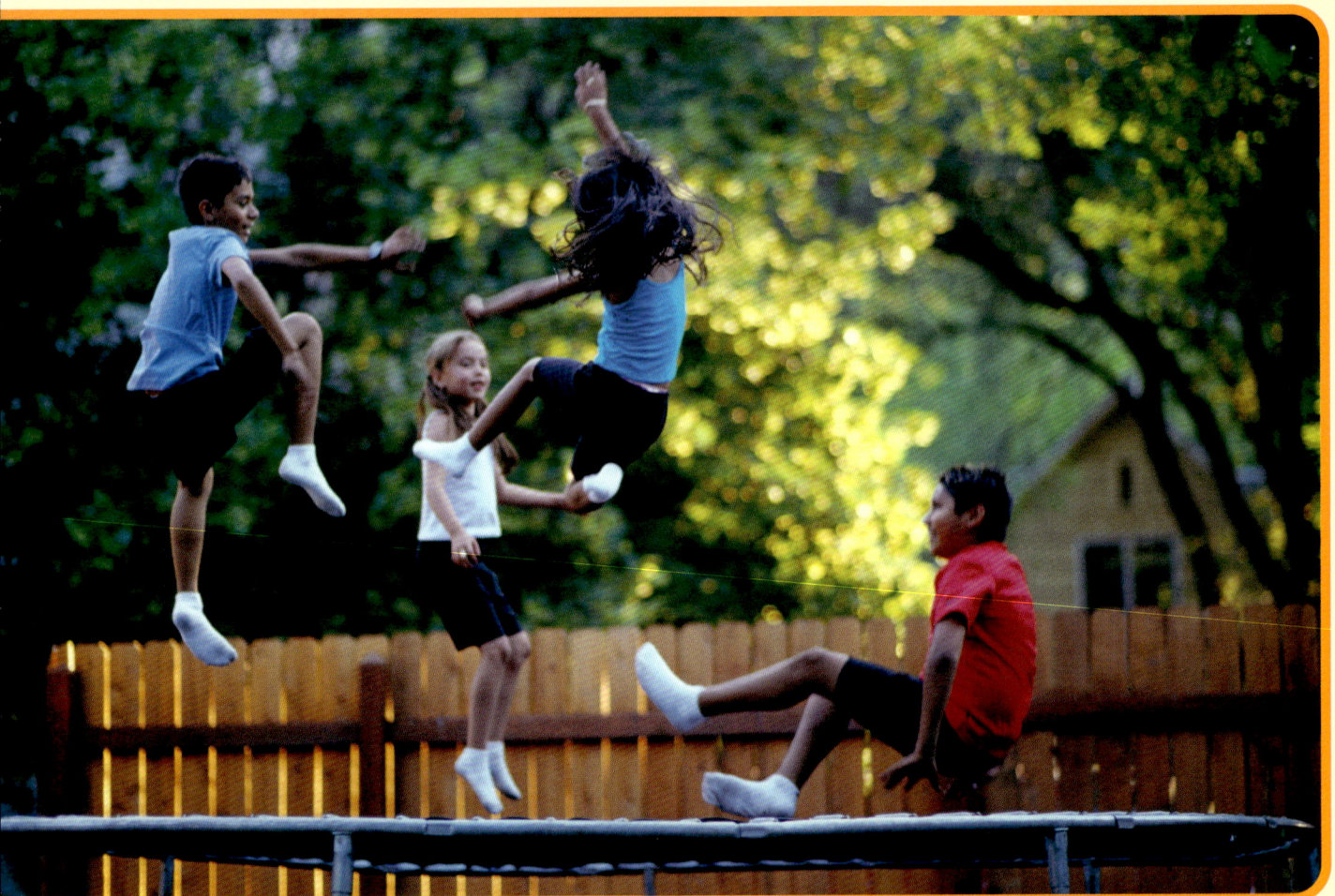

Another sort of energy

Many of the things we do in our homes need energy, too. Have you watched the television, used the computer or gone out in the car today? All of these activities require energy.

Energy in the form of electricity lights our homes and makes many of the appliances, such as the kettle, computer or cooker, work. Cars are also powered by energy, in the form of petrol.

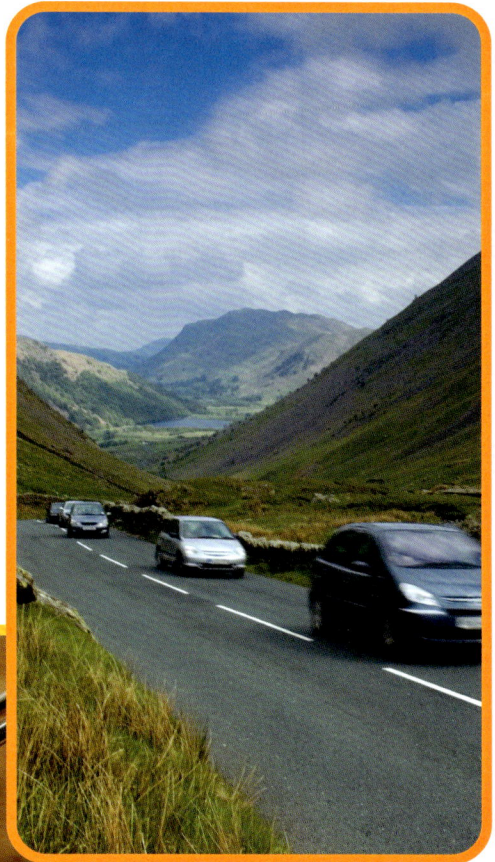

Think of all the things you use energy for in a day. How many of them would you be able to do if you didn't use energy?

Did you know?

People in the US use nearly one million dollars' worth of energy every minute.

Where does energy come from?

So, where does all this energy come from? Well, there are different sources of energy. More than half the world's energy comes from coal, oil and gas.

I know this fuel formed in prehistoric times, but this is ridiculous!

Tidal energy is a clean, renewable form of energy. It is made as tides change from low to high tide.

Fossil fuels

Coal, oil and gas are formed from the remains of plants and animals which have broken down under the ground over millions of years. Because they form underground over a long period of time, they are called **fossil fuels**. There is a limited supply of these fuels because they cannot be replaced, so they are also known as **non-renewable** energy sources.

Sun, sea and wind

Luckily, the Earth has provided us with other types of energy, too. There is solar energy (from the Sun), tidal (from the sea), wind and water power, too. These are known as **renewable** energy sources because they will not run out. However, they cannot be stored easily, so at the moment they are not used as widely as fossil fuels.

If we could store all the sunlight that shines down on the UK in one day, it would be enough to satisfy the UK's electricity needs for two whole years.

In the US, more than 10,000 homes are powered completely by solar energy.

We use solar panels to convert sunlight to energy.

Nuclear power

Nuclear power is another source of energy. It comes from a metal called uranium that is found in the Earth. The metal is split apart into tiny parts called atoms and this process releases energy. The main problem with nuclear energy is that it creates a small amount of very dangerous waste that is difficult to get rid of.

A nuclear power plant in Antwerp, Belgium.

Climate change

The glass in a greenhouse traps and keeps in the Sun's heat. The layer of air around our Earth, called the atmosphere, acts in the same way.

Trapped heat

The atmosphere is made up of different gases, only some of which trap the Sun's heat. They are known as **greenhouse gases** and they contribute to **global warming**. One of the most important of these greenhouse gases is **carbon dioxide** (CO_2). Carbon dioxide is produced when we burn fossil fuels. As we burn more and more fossil fuels to meet our energy needs, the rate of global warming is increasing.

2. Greenhouse gases in the Earth's atmosphere trap some of the Sun's heat. As more fuel is used, more greenhouse gases are added to this layer around the Earth. This means that more heat is kept in, warming the Earth up.

3. Rising temperatures have started to change the weather patterns around the world. This is called **climate change**.

1. Coal, oil and gas develop underground over millions of years. When they are burned, they create energy. Burning these fuels gives off carbon dioxide which is a greenhouse gas.

A change in the weather

As the temperature of the Earth changes, it changes weather patterns around the world. This is called climate change. **Heat waves** and **droughts** are becoming more common in some areas, while rainfall can be very heavy in others, causing flooding. Extreme weather events, such as hurricanes, are also increasing around the world.

Hotting up

The Earth's climate has varied naturally for billions of years, but evidence shows that people have made it change more quickly by burning more and more fossil fuels to provide energy. Out of the five warmest years on record, four have occurred in the last ten years.

Droughts and floods happen all over the world and cause lots of damage.

A BURNING ISSUE

Fossil fuels are used to make 66% of the world's electricity. They are used to create 95% of the energy needed for transport, electricity and heating.

To picture this, imagine a cake cut into three pieces. 66% is two of the three pieces. 95% is nearly the whole cake!

What's your footprint?

Do you know what a '**carbon footprint**' is? Imagine stepping in a muddy puddle, and then walking over a clean, white carpet. Not only would you be in trouble, but you would also leave a trail of footprints behind you.

Footprint trail

A carbon footprint trail is an imaginary trail that we leave when we use electricity, oil and gas in our homes, schools and workplaces, and petrol in our cars and vehicles. Every time we use a 'carbon' energy (coal, oil or gas), it gives off CO_2, and adds to the problem of climate change (see page 11). We are leaving a 'muddy' carbon footprint on the Earth, which can be measured in kilograms of CO_2 released into the air every year.

You can check your carbon footprint by using a footprint calculator on the Internet.

To make and deliver one computer uses over 200 kg of fossil fuel – about the same weight as a fully-grown American black bear!

Direct and indirect

We each have a direct carbon footprint – that's the actual electricity, gas or petrol we use ourselves. But we also have an indirect carbon footprint. That's the energy that has gone into making or transporting something that we use. For example, to make a computer and deliver it to the shop where it will be sold uses over 200 kg of fossil fuels.

A BIG DEMAND

Countries in the developed world, such as the UK and USA, make up about 20% of the world's population, yet they use about 80% of the world's natural resources. This is because where people are richer they tend to buy and use more things, so make more demands on the Earth's resources.

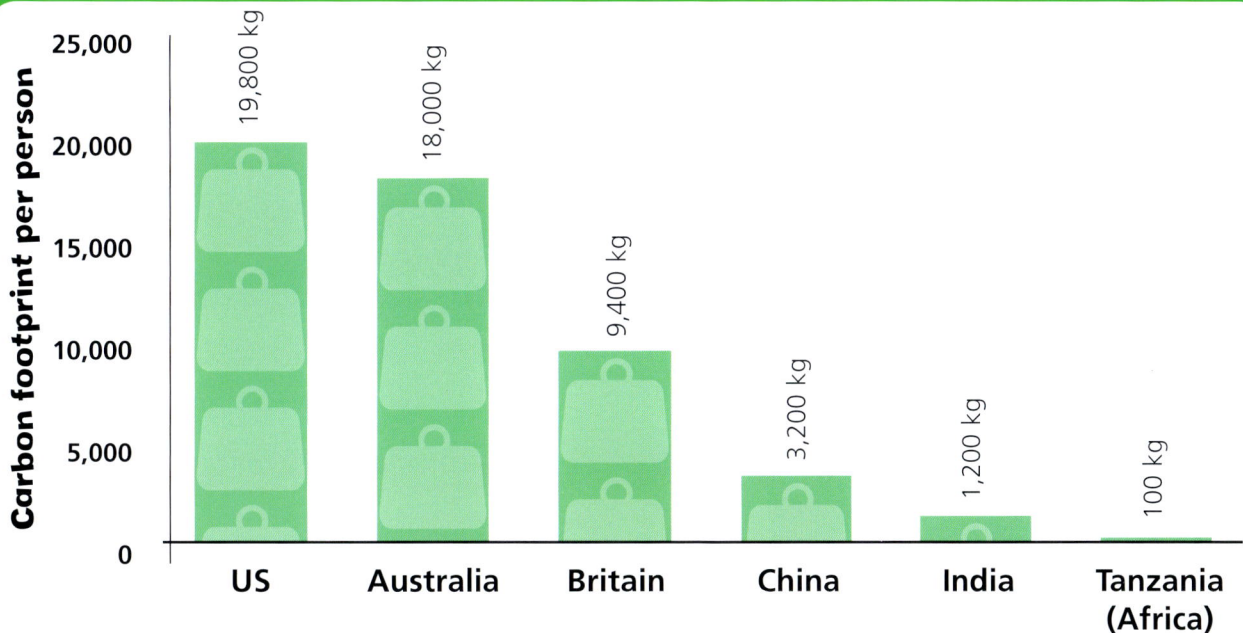

Carbon footprint per person (kg)

Country	Carbon footprint per person
US	19,800 kg
Australia	18,000 kg
Britain	9,400 kg
China	3,200 kg
India	1,200 kg
Tanzania (Africa)	100 kg

One elephant or two?

In the UK, every person has a carbon footprint of nearly 10,000 kg of CO_2. That is the weight of two fully-grown Indian elephants! To stop the Earth heating up any more, this needs to be no more than 3,000 kg per person (less than an elephant each). Each one of us needs to reduce the amount of energy we use.

Developed **countries** such as the US, the UK and Australia have a much bigger carbon footprint than **developing countries** such as Tanzania.

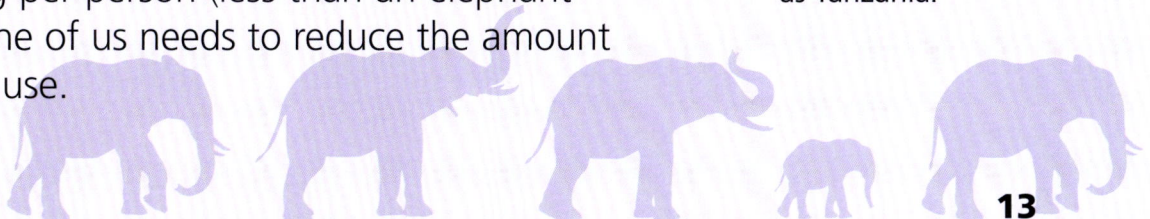

Cut down in the kitchen

The good news is that there are some simple things that each one of us can do to cut down on the energy we use at home, starting in the kitchen. Cutting down on wasting energy saves us money, too, because we pay to use gas and electricity. The less we use, the less we pay.

You can save up to 24 kg of CO_2 a year by using the right amount of water – imagine that as the same weight as 24 bags of sugar!

Less is best

When someone in your house boils the kettle, ask them to heat the smallest amount of water needed. This saves water and uses less energy to heat the water. Over a year, if everyone used only the amount of water needed in the kettle, the UK would save enough electricity to run nearly half the street lamps in the country!

Wash with care

If you help to fill the washing machine or dishwasher, make sure it is only turned on when it is full. Washing the clothes at a lower temperature helps to save energy, too. When it comes to drying the washing, help to hang it up on airers or in the garden. Tumble driers are really expensive to run, both in money and energy terms.

ENERGY STAR

In the US in 2008, Americans saved US $19 billion on energy bills through using products recommended by Energy Star (the energy label). This reduced the amount of greenhouse gases released into the air by the same amount released by 29 million cars.

The appliance of science

If your parents or carer need to replace any of their electrical appliances, such as the washing machine, ask them to look for labels that show their **energy efficiency** rating so that you can choose the most energy efficient model.

Did you know?

Some new refrigerators are so energy efficient that they use less electricity than a light bulb!

Energy labels show which appliances make the best use of energy.

Energy

More efficient

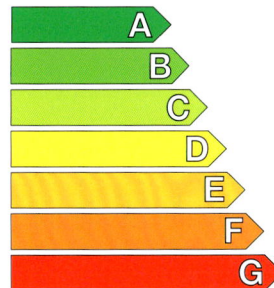

A
B
C
D
E
F
G

Less efficient

A

Light the way

Lights make our homes bright and welcoming, but they also waste a lot of energy through heat. This is especially true of older, traditional light bulbs.

Low-energy bulbs

If every household in the US replaced just one old light bulb with a low-energy light bulb, it would save enough energy to light more than three million homes for a year, and reduce CO_2 **emissions** equivalent to the emissions of 800,000 cars. Low-energy light bulbs last up to 12 times longer than old light bulbs, so they save money as well as CO_2.

Using low-energy light bulbs saves energy, resources and money.

Turning off a light in an empty room for one hour a day for a year saves enough electricity to power your television all evening for a whole month.

You watch, when I flick off the light switch, the TV comes on!

LIGHTENING THE LOAD

By 2015, Australia plans to use only energy-saving light bulbs, saving about 4 million tonnes of CO_2 emissions – the equivalent in weight to 571,429 double-decker buses.

Light housework

Remember to switch off lights in rooms that are not being used. How about helping to clean the windows so you can use as much natural light as possible during the day? It also helps to give light bulbs a dust (when they're cool), as this allows them to give out up to 20% more light.

CASE STUDY

EARTH HOUR

In 2007, the organisation World Wide Fund for Nature started 'Earth Hour' – a campaign to raise awareness about saving energy around the world. Businesses, schools, organisations and homes 'sign up to switch off' their lights and electricity for a set hour, on a set day, at a set time each year. It is an international reminder of how important it is to save energy.

In 2009, more than 1,000 cities in over 80 countries – including Hong Kong (above) – observed Earth Hour.

Keep in the heat

A lot of energy is used to keep our homes warm. Heating can account for up to two-thirds of our total energy use at home.

This picture uses infrared light to show where a house loses its heat. The lightest-coloured parts – such as the door and windows – lose the most heat.

Your parents or carers spend a lot of money on heating your home, so it makes sense to try to make the most of it. Here are some handy energy-saving tips:

- shut the front door quickly when you go in and out to keep in the heat

- put draught excluders by outside doors

- keep the curtains shut, especially in winter

- make sure the curtains don't cover the radiators so heat can move round the room more easily

- help stick foil behind the radiators to reflect the heat back into the house.

Insulation

Over half of the heat from our homes seeps out through the walls and loft. Adding **insulation** to walls and loft spaces can drastically reduce the amount of heat that is lost from your home and saves money on heating bills, too.

Insulating your loft is your home's version of wearing a hat. It helps keep in the warmth!

IT'S GREAT TO INSULATE!

If everyone in the UK added wall insulation to their homes, it would cut the release of CO_2 by a massive 7 million tonnes. That is enough CO_2 to fill a stadium like Wembley 900 times!

Turn it down

Once you've helped to make your house toasty and warm, the biggest way of saving energy in your home is to turn down the temperature on your **thermostat** by 1°C. If you feel a bit chilly every now and then, try putting on a jumper!

Lowering the temperature at home by just 1°C can save about £35 on your heating bill a year, and save around 259.5 kg of CO_2.

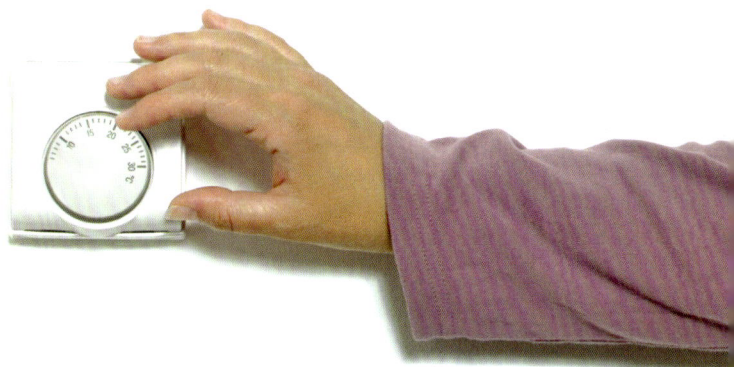

Energy-saving entertainment

Do you like to watch TV and play computer games? How about listening to music? All of these activities use energy.

Think twice! In the UK, two power stations-worth of energy are wasted a year by leaving things on standby.

Rechargeable batteries are better for the environment as they are reused rather than thrown away.

Stand-by

Most of us enjoy watching TV and DVDs. But it's important to remember to switch off electrical appliances when we've finished using them. Did you know that even when something is on standby, it is still really 'on' and using electricity? As a rule, if there's a light on or the gadget feels warm, it is on and using energy.

Recharge your batteries

Just because your computer game is handheld and uses batteries, it doesn't mean that it isn't using energy. Try to use rechargeable batteries in your game. These may be more expensive to buy in the first place, but they work out to be cheaper in the long run, and save on energy, too.

Use your own energy!

Not all activities need to use electricity. How about using your own energy? There are plenty of things to do, both outside and in, that only need your energy. How about playing a game in the garden or park with your friends, riding a bike or scooter, or reading a book?

Did you know?

It takes twice the amount of energy to make an ordinary battery than you can actually get out of a battery.

Remember to check with your parent or carer before you go out for a bike ride.

Recycle and save energy

Many of the things we use are made from natural resources – such as wood or metal. All of the things we use have been made using the Earth's energy supplies.

The three Rs

Have you heard of the three Rs – reduce, reuse and recycle? The three Rs describe how we should treat the things we use, including our toys, books and clothes. It means that we should try to reduce our use of **materials**, reuse materials where we can and, rather than throw things away when we've finished with them, recycle them, so the materials they are made from can be used again.

Recycling saves in two ways: it saves the resources needed to make something new and it saves the energy it takes to make something new.

Did you know?

An 11 watt low-energy light bulb can be powered for 32 hours using the energy saved by recycling one plastic bottle.

Recycling energy

Did you know that by recycling things such as glass, paper, cans and so on, we don't just save the materials that each item is made from, we also save energy? It takes a lot of energy to dig new resources out of the Earth.

We 'can' recycle

The metal aluminium is used to make drinks cans, among other things. It is extracted from the ground. It takes a lot of energy and other resources, such as water, to turn aluminium into a can. However, recycling an aluminium can saves about 90% of the energy used to make the can from new materials – that's saving nearly all the energy used to make a can from new.

Heavy machinery digs into the ground to extract bauxite. This is the mineral in which aluminium is found.

SAVING ENERGY AND THE EARTH

Recycling just one aluminium can saves enough energy to run your TV for three hours.

Recycling nearly one tonne of aluminium saves enough energy to supply a house with electricity for ten years.

Walk, don't ride

There's no getting away from it, travelling by anything that uses fuel rather than our own energy releases a lot of CO_2 into the air.

The cost of travel

In Australia, the emissions from transport make up 15% of greenhouse gases, in the UK it's 25% and in the US over 29%. But many of these journeys are less than eight kilometres long – that would take about half-an-hour on a bike.

Flying high

Air travel contributes a huge amount of these emissions. There are over two flights a second around the world. A big plane like a Boeing 747 uses about four litres of fuel every second. Over a ten hour flight, it will burn about 150,000 litres of fuel. Burning this fuel gives off a lot of carbon dioxide into the air.

Did you know?
A small car will release four to six tonnes of CO_2 into the air in a year – the same weight as a fully grown elephant.

From bike to bus

There is plenty that we can do to reduce transport emissions, though. Where possible, try walking or cycling instead of taking the car. It saves on CO_2 and keeps you fit, too. For longer journeys, travelling by public transport such as the bus reduces emissions. And when it comes to going on holiday, could you get there by boat or train?

Many roads now have lanes that only buses and bicycles can use.

Biofuels v electric

Biofuels are an alternative fuel to petrol. They are made from living plants that are grown and then used to produce energy rather than food. They cancel out the CO_2 they give out when they are burned by using up CO_2 as the plant crops grow. However, it is argued that biofuels use up valuable land that should be used to grow food crops, pushing up world food prices.

When you said it was a short run, I thought you meant a short run in the car!

Every little helps

How we each choose to live directly affects our planet. Energy we use in our homes, driving our cars and by travelling by air makes up 40% of the CO_2 released into the air in some countries – that's nearly half the total CO_2 emissions.

Busy, growing cities need more and more energy.

A growing need

It is all the more important for us to take action now to use less energy because the world's **population** is growing fast. The more of us there are, the more energy we will need. Countries such as India and China are becoming more **industrialised**, as more and more of their population move to the cities to work rather than on farms. This uses yet more energy, and produces yet more CO_2.

CASE STUDY

CARBON TRADING

Governments have had to think about different ways to save energy. One scheme considered was carbon trading. This is a scheme where every company is given a yearly amount of carbon that they can use. Whenever they manufacture a product or use petrol to deliver it, they use up some of their carbon allowance. Those companies that don't use all their allowance can sell their left-over carbon to other companies.

We can do it!

It's not just up to governments to sort this problem out – it's up to us, too. Remember, we each need to use less than an elephant's-worth of energy a year to slow down global warming! We can reduce our energy use by doing simple things like turning the temperature down on our heating and leaving our cars at home.

Write letters to your local MP or mayor to ask what they are doing to develop renewable energy. Remember, if we all make changes to what we do and how we live, we can save money, save energy and reduce the amount of CO_2 in the air.

Can you save an elephant's worth of energy a year? It may be hard work but it will help to save the planet.

Wind turbines generate renewable, clean energy.

Glossary

Carbon dioxide A gas in the air around us.

Carbon footprint The amount of 'carbon' energy (coal, oil or gas) we each use and the amount of carbon dioxide we then contribute to the air.

Climate change Longterm changes to the world's weather patterns.

Developed countries Countries with well-developed economies, where most of the population work in factories and businesses.

Developing countries Countries with less-developed economies, where most of the population work in farming.

Drought A shortage of rain over a long period of time.

Emissions Substances, such as the gas carbon dioxide, that escape into the air.

Energy The power to make or do something.

Energy efficiency Where an appliance, such as a washing machine, does its job in the most efficient way, using the least energy.

Fossil fuels Fuels such as coal, oil or gas, which have developed under the ground from rotting animal and plant life over millions of years.

Global warming The gradual heating up of the Earth's atmosphere.

Greenhouse gas A gas, such as carbon dioxide, that creates an invisible layer around the Earth, keeping in the heat of the Sun's rays.

Heat wave Unusually hot weather in an area over a long period of time.

Industrialised Countries that rely on factories and businesses to create the country's wealth, rather than farming.

Insulate To add an extra layer of material to something to help it keep in heat or keep out cold.

Natural resources Materials, such as water and wood, that are found in nature.

Non-renewable When there is only a certain amount of something, so it will eventually run out.

Materials What something is made from, such as cotton, wood or metal, for example.

Population The number of people living in a place.

Renewable Something that is in constant supply and will not run out, such as the wind.

Thermostat The controls that set the temperature for a heating system.

Useful information

Throughout this book, 'real life measurements' are used for reference. These measurements are not exact, but give a sense of just how much an amount of energy is, or what it looks like.

Bag of sugar = 1 KG

American black bear = 270 kg

Fully-grown Indian elephant = 5,000 KG or 5 tonnes

Double decker bus = 7,000 KG or 7 tonnes

Further reading

How Can We Save Our World? Sustainable Energy by Angela Royston (Franklin Watts, 2009)

Science on the Edge: Alternative Energy Sources by Sally Morgan (Heinemann, 2009)

Green Team: Using Energy by Sally Hewitt (Franklin Watts, 2008)

Websites

www.biggreenswitch.co.uk
News, views and advice on all things green.

www.eco-schools.co.uk
An awards scheme set up to help UK schools save energy.

www.energysavingtrust.org.uk
Tips and advice on saving energy.

Dates to remember

Earth Hour – 28 March

Earth Day – 22 April

World Environment Day – 5 June

Clean Air Day – June

Walk to School Campaign – May and October

World Food Day – 16 October

Buy Nothing Day – 28 November

Note to parents and teachers: Every effort has been made by the Publishers to ensure that these websites are suitable for children, that they are of the highest educational value, and that they contain no inappropriate or offensive material. However, because of the nature of the Internet, it is impossible to guarantee that the contents of these sites will not be altered. We strongly advise that Internet access is supervised by a responsible adult

Index